CLEAN

I0139811

Edwin Sánchez

BROADWAY PLAY PUBLISHING INC
New York
www.broadwayplaypublishing.com
info@broadwayplaypublishing.com

CLEAN
© Copyright 1997 by Edwin Sánchez

CLEAN was first published in a collection entitled *Plays By Edwin Sanchez* in February 1997

First printing, this edition December 2010
I S B N: 978-0-88145-488-8

Book design: Marie Donovan
Page make-up: Adobe Indesign
Typeface: Palatino
Printed and bound in the U S A

ABOUT THE AUTHOR

Recent productions include TRAFFICKING IN
BROKEN HEARTS at the Celebration Theater in Los
Angeles as well as the world premiere of his romantic
comedy I'LL TAKE ROMANCE at the Evolution
Theater in Ohio. His newest play LA BELLA FAMILIA
will be produced by Teatro Vista in Chicago in
2011. Other productions include, DIOSA, produced
by Hartford Stage after a successful workshop
by New York Stage and Film, TRAFFICKING IN
BROKEN HEARTS at the Atlantic Theater in New
York, UNMERCIFUL GOOD FORTUNE at the Intar
Theater in New York, ICARUS produced by Fourth
Unity in New York, Actors Theater of Louisville as
part of their Humana Festival, and San Jose Rep in
California. His play BAREFOOT BOY WITH SHOES
ON was produced by Primary Stages in New York
and was selected by the Eugene O'Neill Playwrights
Conference to represent the National Playwrights
Conference at the Schelykovo Playwrights Seminar
in Russia. Mr Sanchez' work has been produced
regionally throughout the United States as well as
Brazil and Switzerland. Among his awards are the
Kennedy Center Fund for New American Plays
(CLEAN), three New York Foundation for the Arts
Playwriting/Screenwriting Fellowships, the Princess
Grace Playwriting Fellowship (UNMERCIFUL
GOOD FORTUNE), the Daryl Roth Creative Spirit

Award and the A T & T On Stage New Play Award
(UNMERCIFUL GOOD FORTUNE). Mr Sanchez lives
in upstate New York where he continues to write as
well as teach and mentors playwrights.

CLEAN premiered at The Hartford Stage (Mark Lamos, Artistic Director; Stephen Albert, Managing Director) on 25 March 1995. The cast and creative contributors were:

GUSTAVITO .... Joe Quintero
MERCY .... Paula Pizzi
KIKO.. Mateo Gomez
FATHER .... Neil Maffin
JUNIOR .... Nelson Vasquez
NORRY .... A Benard Cummings

Director .... Graciela Daniele
Set design .... Christopher Barreca
Costume design .... Eduardo Sicangco
Light design .... David F Segal
Sound design .... David Budries
Original music .... Robert C Cotnoir
Production dramaturg .... Kim Euell
Casting .... Bernard Telsey Casting
Production stage manager .... Barbara Reo
Assistant stage manager .... Deborah Vandergrift

This play was originally produced with the assistance of the Fund for New American Plays, a project of the John F Kennedy Center for the Performing Arts, with support from American Express Company in cooperation with the President's Committee on the Arts and Humanities.

CHARACTERS & SETTING

FATHER
MERCY
KIKO
JUNIOR
GUSTAVITO
NORRY

GUSTAVITO *is 7 and* JUNIOR *is 12 at the beginning of the play. The action takes place during the course of eight years.*

The first act takes place in the Bronx, NY. The second act takes place in the Bronx and Puerto Rico.

ACT ONE

(The stage is dark. A giant cross begins to glow. It takes up most of the stage and is located in the center. One key of music is heard; the cross rises. Standing behind the brilliant, white cross is GUSTAVITO, *age 7, played by an adult actor and wearing only his jockey shorts. He runs to the edge of the stage. He is the only figure we see in a pool of light.)*

GUSTAVITO: *(Sings)*
Two and time
follow me
to the bottom of the sea.
While you're there
wash your hair
and your dirty underwear.

MERCY: *(Voice only)* Gustavito, you had better get yourself—

GUSTAVITO: *(Sings)*	MERCY:
Two and tie	—into this bath tub.
follow me	
to the bottom of the sea.	
While you're there	
wash your hair	I'm not kidding with you
and your dirty underwear.	

(The lights come up to reveal a small bathroom. MERCY *is kneeling by the bath tub.* GUSTAVITO *gets into the bath tub, still wearing his underwear.)*

MERCY: My dirty, little man.

(She begins to bathe him.)

GUSTAVITO: Mercy, don't touch my thing.

MERCY: Nobody want to touch that dirty thing. It smells. *(She puts her hand in the water and grabs him, takes out her hand and smells it.)* Oooh, stinky.

GUSTAVITO: Nah-uh.

(She kisses the top of his head.)

MERCY: Mercy's dirty, little boy.

(The sound of a door opening and closing is heard. KIKO has arrived.)

KIKO: *(Voice only)* Mercedes!

(MERCY locks the bathroom door. She takes a hammer, which has been sitting on the toilet seat, and holds it in her hand.)

KIKO: Mercedes! Can't you hear your Kiko calling you?

(GUSTAVITO goes underwater.)

MERCY: Gustavito. Gustavito.

(GUSTAVITO emerges.)

GUSTAVITO: Is Kiko mad?

MERCY: Take off your underwear, no he's not mad, and wash it. Like this.

(She puts the hammer on her lap and mimes washing clothing by rubbing her fists against each other. KIKO begins to bang against the door. MERCY flinches, but continues.)

KIKO: Goddamn it, I gotta take a shit, Mercedes!

(MERCY picks up the hammer. She takes out a magazine and begins to look through it.)

MERCY: I'll make you a nice birthday cake and we'll put seven candles on it, with one for luck. Two and time, follow me... Come on, Gustavito.

(GUSTAVITO softly sings his song.)

KIKO: Open the fucking door, Mercedes! *(He begins to pound on the door.* MERCY *puts the magazine down and stands by attention at the door, hammer poised in mid-air.)* Mercedes!

MERCY: To the bottom of the sea.

*(*GUSTAVITO *begins to wash his underwear.)*

GUSTAVITO: While you're there wash your hair and your dirty underwear. I'm scared.

MERCY: If he really wanted to get in he would.

KIKO: *(Softly)* Mercedes.

GUSTAVITO: While you're there—

MERCY: All he has to do is turn the knob.

GUSTAVITO: —wash your hair...big bubble.

*(*GUSTAVITO *hums the rest of the song.* MERCY *is lovingly tracing a heart on the door with the hammer. The sudden silence brings her from her reverie. She tries to get him singing again.)*

MERCY: And your dirty.

GUSTAVITO: Un-der-wear.

(A church confessional. GUSTAVITO *enters and takes a seat in the penitent's side. He is wearing a baseball cap.)*

GUSTAVITO: Forgive me Father, for I have sinned. This is my first confession.

FATHER: Yes, go ahead my son.

GUSTAVITO: I stole a hat, a baseball cap.

FATHER: From where?

GUSTAVITO: From Woolworth's.

FATHER: You have to take it back.

GUSTAVITO: I can't. *(He takes off the cap.)* I lost it.

FATHER: Forgiveness will only come if you pay for your sins.

GUSTAVITO: I'm real sorry. I don't have any money. They dared me to do it.

FATHER: Who did?

GUSTAVITO: Some friends.

FATHER: Those aren't your friends.

GUSTAVITO: I can get the money from Mercy.

FATHER: She wasn't the one who stole it.

GUSTAVITO: I won't do it again.

FATHER: What did you do with the hat?

GUSTAVITO: I didn't even want it. I was so scared I just threw it away. Sister Frances at school, she started telling us about Hell and how terrible it is. I don't want to go there. Help me, please.

FATHER: I want you to say three Our Fathers and think about what you did. Will you promise me you'll never steal again?

GUSTAVITO: Uh-huh. Can you see me?

FATHER: What?

GUSTAVITO: Can you see me? I can't see you.

(FATHER *crosses himself. Lights down.*)

(KIKO *is asleep in his armchair. He is snoring loudly.*
MERCY *and* GUSTAVITO *enter.* GUSTAVITO *sits at* KIKO's
feet and very tenderly and slowly removes KIKO's *shoes and
socks through the course the scene.*)

MERCY: (*Almost to herself.*) I don't know when I'm going, but I'm going.

GUSTAVITO: He gets corns on his feet. They're very rough. He must have walked barefoot a lot.

MERCY: He was barefoot when I first met him. Pant legs rolled up, in the river behind our house. Consuelo and me, we first saw him together.

GUSTAVITO: I've seen him cut off the corns with a razor. He draws blood sometimes. He wanted to teach me how to do it, but I hid. No way.

MERCY: *(Sweetly) Pendejo.*

GUSTAVITO: *Pendeja tu.*

MERCY: Do you miss your mother? Just now, that little pout reminded me of her.

GUSTAVITO: I don't remember her.

MERCY: Esperanza wasn't even with us when we saw Kiko. What a shameless man. To marry all three sisters. And when he came for me, I was going to be different. I was going to stand in that doorway and chase him away. Instead, I had my bag packed the night before. Maybe he was the price the Gomez sisters had to pay to leave their family. I'll tell you a little secret. You were supposed to be mine. Kiko married Consuelo first, although for a long time I don't think he knew which one he liked better. Then, he chose Esperanza. I came in a very distant third.

GUSTAVITO: It wasn't a contest, Mercy.

MERCY: Oh yes it was. Consuelo got him then Esperanza got him and I got to take care of my parents. And do you know, when Consuelo passed on—

GUSTAVITO: Died.

MERCY: —went to Heaven, and Esperanza escaped to God-knows-where, Kiko comes with his hat in his hand to see if I'm available. If I'm available.

GUSTAVITO: You were waiting for him.

MERCY: To punish him. *(She mimes locking her lips with a key.)* We have been together for seven years and I have never let him touch me. And he won't.

GUSTAVITO: Don't you want him to touch you?

MERCY: Give me his socks, I'll wash them.

GUSTAVITO: That's my job. I wear them like gloves and let the water run and wash my hands.

MERCY: You leave too much soap in them.

GUSTAVITO: I do not. *(Pause)* Don't you want him to touch you?

(MERCY exits. GUSTAVITO remains crouched at KIKO's feet.)

GUSTAVITO: So today at school we had a spelling bee and I won so I got a star by my name. A star means I'm good.

(KIKO snores as he changes positions.)

GUSTAVITO: And Jose Manuel wanted to wait outside for me and beat me up 'cause he said I was showing off. I told him you would come in and beat him up if he did...I stole something today.

(In the now-empty church, GUSTAVITO approaches FATHER.)

GUSTAVITO: Father. I waited for you.

(FATHER looks at him quizzically.)

GUSTAVITO: I'm the one who stole the baseball cap.

FATHER: Ah. You were here with your mother. Where is she?

GUSTAVITO: She's not my mother. She's Mercy. She don't like going to church so she always crochets. She's going to go to Hell, right, Father?

FATHER: That's not exactly how it works. So, did you tell your father what you did?

GUSTAVITO: Oh, he forgave me. That was a nice Mass you did. How old were you when you knew you wanted to be a priest?

FATHER: About your age I guess.

GUSTAVITO: Who did you tell?

FATHER: My parents.

GUSTAVITO: Were they proud that God had chosen you?

FATHER: God didn't choose me, I chose Him.

GUSTAVITO: Same thing.

FATHER: *(Sharply)* No, there's a very big difference.

GUSTAVITO: Okay, okay, there's a very big difference. I bet I can tell you what you were like at my age.

FATHER: Bet you can't.

GUSTAVITO: You were a lot like me, I think I'm more curiouser, though.

FATHER: Curious. Do you have a lot of friends?

GUSTAVITO: No, not really. Uh, no.

FATHER: Maybe you are like me at your age.

GUSTAVITO: A priest job would be perfect for me. What do you do all day? Pray and listen to secrets.

FATHER: They're not secrets, they're sins. I'll tell you what, I'll bring you a little book next week, okay?

GUSTAVITO: For me?

FATHER: Yeah, for you. You see another thief around here? *(He pulls the baseball cap from GUSTAVITO's back pocket.)* I'm kidding.

GUSTAVITO: But not about the book, right?

FATHER: No, not about the book.

GUSTAVITO: I'll see you next week then.

(GUSTAVITO *runs out. He has left the baseball cap behind.*)

(*The Delgado living room*)

KIKO: Te voy a decir la purisima verdad. I am going to tell you the purest of truths. "Purest of truths". Not diluted by lies, not even a little bit. (*He shuffles a deck of cards and quickly sets out the cards for a game of solitaire. He speeds through the deck, to hurry along the game. His game is not about rules, it is about speed.*)

JUNIOR: Anytime today.

KIKO: God invented love to punish people.

JUNIOR: Good night.

(KIKO *has gone as far as he can with this game. He collects the cards and shuffles them as before and begins again.*)

KIKO: You see Mercy? I love Mercy. Don't I, honey?

(MERCY *does not look up from her sewing.*)

MERCY: The word loses all value in your mouth.

KIKO: (*To* JUNIOR) And I loved your mother, Consuelo. (To GUSTAVITO) And I even had enough love left over to love your mother, Gustavito.

GUSTAVITO: Mami Esperanza.

KIKO: You know I'm talking to you 'cause I care.

JUNIOR: He's drunk out of his mind.

KIKO: I would rather be in love than anything.

GUSTAVITO: And if they don't love you back?

KIKO: All the better. Right, Mercy?

(MERCY *ignores him.*)

KIKO: Right.

JUNIOR: Shit, a woman don't know I love her I make her know.

(MERCY *gives him a condescending look.*)

JUNIOR: It's the truth. (*To* GUSTAVITO, *referring to* KIKO) Weak man.

KIKO: (*Referring to his game*) A spade is a spade.

JUNIOR: Don't know how to carry his balls. Hope you didn't turn out the same way. If you love somebody, they belong to you. Period. That's how it is. You see Mercy? She belong to Kiko.

GUSTAVITO: You full of shit.

(KIKO *takes his card table to* MERCY *so that she can see his game. She does not look up.* KIKO *exits.* JUNIOR *takes* GUSTAVITO'*s middle finger and folds it back.* GUSTAVITO *winces in pain.*)

JUNIOR: Shut up so you can hear the sound of the bone breaking.

GUSTAVITO: Mercy.

(MERCY *looks up.*)

JUNIOR: (*Under his breath*) Crack.

(GUSTAVITO *is silent.* MERCY *exits.*)

JUNIOR: Who's full of shit?

GUSTAVITO: I am.

JUNIOR: And who's not?

GUSTAVITO: You.

JUNIOR: You're gonna be just like Kiko. The ball-less wonder. (*He exits.*)

(GUSTAVITO *gets on his knees in prayer. Lights dim so that only a dim light remains on him. Lights slowly begin to come up as* KIKO *enters, dressed for work and with his lunch pail. He looks at* GUSTAVITO, *shakes his head, and exits.*

Lights slowly come up to full. A knock is heard. MERCY *enters in a disheveled house dress and her hair uncombed.)*

GUSTAVITO: Amen. *(Crossing himself and running to the door.)*

MERCY: Don't you dare open that door, Gustavito.

*(*GUSTAVITO *opens the door to reveal* NORRY, *who is wearing an evening dress. He is in full make-up.)*

GUSTAVITO: Uyy. *(He runs and hides behind* MERCY.*)*

NORRY: Aren't you just the cutest little thing?

*(*GUSTAVITO *shakes his head from behind* MERCY.*)*

NORRY: Well, suit yourself. *(To* MERCY*)* Mercedes La Milagrosa?

MERCY: Yes. *(She tries to make herself more presentable.)*

NORRY: You're the seamstress who can do anything, huh?

MERCY: Yes. I'm sorry, come in.

*(*NORRY *enters)*

GUSTAVITO: *(To* MERCY*)* He's pretty.

MERCY: Sssh.

NORRY: No baby, I'm beautiful. My imitators are pretty. I want to hire you, Mercy.

MERCY: Call me Mercy.

NORRY: Money is no object as long as it doesn't cost more that a hundred dollars.

MERCY: I...I make dresses for women.

NORRY: I want a wedding dress.

MERCY: I don't think so.

NORRY: A mother fucking kind of wedding dress. *(He sits in one, sweeping, graceful movement.)* Do you have any coffee?

MERCY: No.

NORRY: A Puerto Rican house without coffee? Rebel.

MERCY: *(Smiles)* Gustavito, get lost.

NORRY: Comadre.

(GUSTAVITO pretends to leave, but hides behind a chair.)

NORRY: I'm thinking of something with lots of low cut, you know what I'm saying? Tight here *(Points to breasts)* and tight here *(Waist)* and Honey, very tight here. *(Hips)*

MERCY: This is a wedding dress?

NORRY: This is Norry's wedding dress.

MERCY: Well, Norry, I don't think my husband is going to like you here.

NORRY: And you always do what he says.

MERCY: You'd have to be here for fittings.

NORRY: I've been collecting white things to sew on this dress. Since forever.

MERCY: And Junior won't like it.

NORRY: It's for an act I do at the Red Castle. Nice little dive where my reign as Queen Bee is being threatened by a bunch of back-stabbing bitches who just recently lost the training wheels on their spike heels.

MERCY: English or Spanish, but this I don't understand.

(Enter JUNIOR. MERCY rises, sensing trouble ahead.)

MERCY: Uh, Junior, I need you to go to the store for me.

JUNIOR: Send the midget.

(NORRY reaches into his purse and gives JUNIOR some money.)

NORRY: Get me a beer and get yourself one, too.

(JUNIOR *is about to take the money. He stops and eyes* NORRY.)

JUNIOR: Hey, wait a second. You ain't no woman.

NORRY: It's okay. You're not a man, yet.

MERCY: Uh, Norry.

JUNIOR: Get your faggot ass outta this house. Now. Ahora.

NORRY: *(Dismissing* JUNIOR *and turning his attention to* MERCY*)* And I figured before the wedding dress we would do a showgirl outfit. Very Ann Margret. Right?

(JUNIOR *grabs* NORRY's *arm and yanks him up.*)

JUNIOR: You're fucked.

NORRY: Okay, Papito, but you had better be ready to kill me 'cause with whatever you leave I will scrape it together and cut your cojones off and wear them for earrings.

(JUNIOR *pushes* NORRY, *who kicks off his heels.* MERCY *gets between them.*)

MERCY: Hey, hey, hey, hey.

NORRY: Let the boy try. As a man or as a woman I am too too much for him.

(KIKO *enters.* GUSTAVITO *peeks over from behind the chair and crosses himself.*)

KIKO: Mercy. *(To* NORRY*)* Doñita. I wasn't expecting company.

NORRY: Norry. Norry Del Alma.

MERCY: She wants me to sew for her.

KIKO: Your humble servant.

JUNIOR: Hello? It's a man in a dress. Hello?

(KIKO *slaps* JUNIOR.)

KIKO: In this house we respect our guests. He is wearing a dress so in this house he's a she. *(He takes off his belt and folds in menacingly.)* You understand me?

(JUNIOR makes a blustery show of heading to the door.)

JUNIOR: Let me see if I can invite more freaks into this fucking house.

(KIKO slams JUNIOR against the wall. He takes him by the hair and slams his head against the wall.)

MERCY: Kiko, por favor.

KIKO: The question, "You understand me?"

JUNIOR: Yeah.

(KIKO lets JUNIOR go.)

KIKO: Go out for an hour.

(JUNIOR exits, looking down at the floor.)

MERCY: One of these days you're gonna hurt that boy, Kiko. I think that's why he's crazy.

KIKO: Don't worry. I'll beat the craziness out of him.

(NORRY looks from KIKO to MERCY.)

NORRY: *(Awkwardly)* I seem to be barefoot.

(KIKO offers his arm as NORRY gets back in his heels.)

MERCY: So you were saying showgirl, right?

NORRY: Huh?

MERCY: You'll want a head dress.

NORRY: Yeah. To the sky. Or so I can wear it on the subway.

MERCY: I've never made a head dress before.

NORRY: I'll help you.

KIKO: Mercy, have you offered our guest any refreshment?

MERCY: I'm the hostess! I know when I have to offer stuff! *(To* NORRY*)* You want some Tang?

KIKO: Go make some Tang for us.

NORRY: Just a little bit. That would be nice, yeah.

*(*MERCY *exits.)*

KIKO: Gustavito, come on, stop hiding. Everybody's seen you already. Take off my shoes.

*(*GUSTAVITO *emerges from his hiding place and begins to take off* KIKO*'s shoes.)*

NORRY: You must be on your feet all day, huh? My father was a, was a, was a waiter so he was always on his feet. What do you do, Don Kiko?

*(*KIKO *motions* NORRY *to lean in.)*

KIKO: In my house, my family is sacred. You don't disrespect me or my family.

NORRY: I would never do that.

*(*KIKO *holds up his hand to silence* NORRY*.)*

KIKO: Outside of this house you can set fire to yourself for all I care, but here, no. You don't come here when my children are here and you are only allowed to sit in the living room. You don't cross that doorway. *(Points to doorway leading to the rest of the apartment)* You want Mercy to sew for you, okay. But you remember, you have no friends here.

(The Rectory. GUSTAVITO *is showing the* FATHER *pictures. The first is of the Delgado men in their Sunday best.)*

GUSTAVITO: This is Kiko and my brother Junior. *(The next shot is of* KIKO *and* JUNIOR*. They both have beers in their hands.)* Junior's not supposed to drink yet, but... *(The next shot is of* MERCY *and* GUSTAVITO*.)* This is Mercy and me.

FATHER: She your mother?

GUSTAVITO: No.

FATHER: Is she Junior's mother?

GUSTAVITO: No.

(The next shot is of KIKO *and* MERCY. *They appear ill at ease.)*

GUSTAVITO: This is Kiko and Mercy.

FATHER: Is she your father's sister?

GUSTAVITO: No, she's his wife. They just don't like each other.

(The next shot is of MERCY. *She is alone and is wearing a cocktail dress. Her hair and make-up are done and she looks seductively into the camera.)*

GUSTAVITO: I'm not supposed to show that one. All the rest are like that. Pretty shots. She likes that. Kinda sexy.

FATHER: You have a very handsome family.

GUSTAVITO: Yeah. Thank you, I mean. Here. *(He gives him a picture.)* That's me. You can keep it.

FATHER: No, I can't do that. They belong to your family.

GUSTAVITO: It's okay. I'll tell them I lost it.

*(*FATHER *playfully hits* GUSTAVITO *on the head with the picture.)*

FATHER: You're not supposed to lie, remember.

GUSTAVITO: They won't mind I gave it to you.

*(*FATHER *looks at the picture once again.)*

FATHER: You'll let me know if they want it back?

*(*GUSTAVITO *nods. Silence)*

GUSTAVITO: Do you think Mercy's pretty?

FATHER: Yes, she's very pretty.

(GUSTAVITO *tries to imitate one of* MERCY's *poses.*)

GUSTAVITO: Do you think we look alike?

FATHER: ...No.

GUSTAVITO: I do. Thank you again for the book.

FATHER: Now you read it, okay?

GUSTAVITO: Yeah. You're real nice, you know.

FATHER: Just doing my job.

GUSTAVITO: Oh.

FATHER: I'll see you in Mass.

GUSTAVITO: Is it okay if I come to visit you?

FATHER: Sure.

GUSTAVITO: Do you want me to come and visit you? I gotta go. Can I have a picture of you? Bring it tomorrow, okay.

(GUSTAVITO *runs out.* JUNIOR *is waiting for him outside.*)

JUNIOR: You get lost in there?

GUSTAVITO: Sorry. (*He starts looking through his book.*)

JUNIOR: What's that?

GUSTAVITO: A book. The Father gave it to me.

JUNIOR: Why would he give you anything?

GUSTAVITO: I gave him a picture of me. We sorta traded. He likes me. A lot.

(JUNIOR *stops* GUSTAVITO.)

JUNIOR: Go get the picture back—

GUSTAVITO: I'm not gonna (*do that*)

JUNIOR: —and give him back his book.

GUSTAVITO: No.

(JUNIOR *takes the book from* GUSTAVITO, *who begins to hit him.*)

GUSTAVITO: Give it back to me.

(JUNIOR *throws the book on the floor.*)

GUSTAVITO: Mother fucker.

(GUSTAVITO *tries to go for the book but* JUNIOR *twists* GUSTAVITO'*s arm behind his back.*)

GUSTAVITO: I'm gonna tell Kiko.

JUNIOR: Yeah, tell him so he can come down to the church and kill the priest. (*He kisses* GUSTAVITO'*s head, even as he holds his arm.*) If Kiko starts thinking there's something wrong he'll kill you, Gustavito. I'm not bullshitting. And ain't Mercy or me gonna be able to stop him.

GUSTAVITO: I didn't do nothing.

JUNIOR: Did the Father do anything to you?

GUSTAVITO: No, asshole.

(JUNIOR *twists his arm again.*)

GUSTAVITO: Ow, no, Junior.

JUNIOR: Promise me you'll never come here again. Promise.

GUSTAVITO: Break the mother fucking arm.

(JUNIOR *pushes* GUSTAVITO *away.* GUSTAVITO *picks up the book.*)

JUNIOR: I'm gonna give you a head start, then I'm gonna take that book and throw it away.

(GUSTAVITO *runs off.* FATHER *is getting into his car.* JUNIOR *surprises him and gets in on the passenger side. He has an unlit cigarette behind his ear.*)

JUNIOR: Yo, Padre.

(FATHER *stares at him for a moment.*)

JUNIOR: Going for a little ride? Good. I'm in the mood to travel. Put it in gear.

FATHER: Get out of the car.

JUNIOR: You know, even if you're parking on church property you should lock this baby up. People like to take what don't belong to them sometimes.

FATHER: Then I'm getting out.

(FATHER *tries to leave;* JUNIOR *grabs his arm.*)

JUNIOR: I'm paying you a visit, Father.

FATHER: I don't think so.

JUNIOR: Then consider this my confession. I think I want to kill you.

(FATHER *looks at* JUNIOR.)

JUNIOR: And that's a sin. But touching Gustavito is a sin, too. Isn't it?

(FATHER *swallows.*)

JUNIOR: I'm not getting an answer here. Hello? It's a sin, isn't it? *(Silence)* Have you touched him?

FATHER: *(Softly)* No.

JUNIOR: But you want to.

FATHER: I have never touched your brother.

JUNIOR: Well, I hope so for your sake. `Cause I will kill you and this is not a threat, this is a fact. You hear what I'm saying?

(FATHER *nods.*)

JUNIOR: I don't think you should see him again. I don't think your filthy eyes should ever gaze on my little brother again. *(He puts his cigarette in his mouth and pushes in the car cigarette lighter. Silence)*

FATHER: He likes to come to the church.

JUNIOR: *(Cutting him off)* —because you are scum.

(Silence. The lighter pops up and JUNIOR *lights his cigarette. He holds the lighter for a second and then holds it inches away from the* FATHER's *face.* FATHER *is taken by surprise; he tries to move away but is trapped in the car.)*

JUNIOR: You would still have another eye. My brother ain't no faggot. My brother ain't never gonna be no faggot and if you make him one you'll have to deal with me. And I ain't God, I don't forgive. *(He puts the lighter back.)* So what's my penance?

FATHER: An act of kindness. That's all it was. Something I would have done for any child.

JUNIOR: Three hail Marys and all is forgiven? Thank you, Father. *(He gets out of the car.)*

FATHER: You're very wrong. I don't have any feelings for your brother.

*(*JUNIOR *exits.* FATHER *sits motionless for a second. He opens the car door and vomits.)*

(Living room. GUSTAVITO *lays out a towel on the sofa and sits next to it. The wedding dress on the sewing dummy is in its earliest stages.* MERCY *is hard at work on it.)*

KIKO: *(Referring to the towel)* What's that for?

GUSTAVITO: This is for God to sit.

KIKO: What he say?

MERCY: Leave him alone. He thinks God is sitting next to him.

KIKO: Saint Gustavito, huh?

MERCY: He goes to church every day.

JUNIOR: What do you do there all the time?

*(*GUSTAVITO *holds up his hand to stop him. He finishes praying.)*

GUSTAVITO: I pray.

JUNIOR: You're just a kid, what the fuck do you have to pray about?

(KIKO *gets up. It should appear that he is about to hit* JUNIOR.)

JUNIOR: What do you have to pray about. That's what I meant to say.

MERCY: Kiko, please.

JUNIOR: Quit hanging out in church, Gustavito. It looks bad.

(KIKO *exits into the kitchen.*)

MERCY: You got a filthy mind.

(KIKO *enters with a grater. He places it on the floor.*)

KIKO: *(To* JUNIOR*)* Kneel on it.

(MERCY *puts down her sewing.* GUSTAVITO *goes back to praying.* JUNIOR *slowly rises and is about to kneel on the grater.*)

KIKO: Lower your pants. Bare knees.

(JUNIOR *does. He kneels on the grater.*)

MERCY: This is why Esperanza left, Kiko.

KIKO: Nobody's holding you here. You leave today, I'll have somebody else tomorrow. *(To* JUNIOR*)* You stay there until midnight.

(KIKO *and* MERCY *exit.* GUSTAVITO'S *prayer slowly becomes louder. For the last line he is joined by* JUNIOR.)

JUNIOR & GUSTAVITO: ...now in the hour of our death, amen.

(GUSTAVITO *rises and enters the confessional.*)

GUSTAVITO: Forgive me Father, for I have sinned. It's me, Gustavito.

FATHER: You've got to be careful when you come here.

GUSTAVITO: I know, Junior. He's like watching me all the time. Asshole.

FATHER: What did you tell him?

GUSTAVITO: I didn't tell him nothing.

FATHER: Don't get into any trouble because of me.

GUSTAVITO: Hey, he's not my father. He's not you.

FATHER: Gustavito, I'm not your father.

GUSTAVITO: You're better than my father. I don't have to be afraid of you.

FATHER: You love Kiko, right?

GUSTAVITO: ...Yeah.

FATHER: He loves you very much.

GUSTAVITO: How do you know?

FATHER: Put your palm on the screen.

(GUSTAVITO *places his palm against the* FATHER'*s.*)

FATHER: I'm going to close my eyes, you close yours.

GUSTAVITO: Okay. Now what?

FATHER: I'll tell you a secret. Nobody can see us in here.

GUSTAVITO: I know that. That ain't no secret.

FATHER: No, I mean, you can't see me and I really can't see you. We're together, we're touching, but we can't see each other.

GUSTAVITO: Are you ashamed of me?

FATHER: No. Don't ever think that.

GUSTAVITO: Clap your hand against mine.

(FATHER *and* GUSTAVITO *clap palms.*)

GUSTAVITO: Make a wish. (*He exits confessional.*)

FATHER: I wish I were you.

GUSTAVITO: Can I try on your rosary?

FATHER: It's not a toy.

GUSTAVITO: That's okay. I'm not playing.

(FATHER *hesitates, begins to remove his rosary.*)

GUSTAVITO: What does it mean when you dream about somebody?

(FATHER *stops.*)

FATHER: What did you dream of?

GUSTAVITO: God. He was just floating there. Not saying anything. No expression on His face. But if I squinted my eyes—rosary, Father—

(FATHER *removes his rosary and holds it over* GUSTAVITO's *head.*)

GUSTAVITO: —if I squinted my eyes I could pretend He was smiling.

(FATHER *is about to place the rosary around* GUSTAVITO's *neck.*)

GUSTAVITO: Hold it a second. (*He pulls out his shirt tails in an effort to imitate the* FATHER's *alb. He kneels.*) Go ahead.

(FATHER *places rosary.*)

GUSTAVITO: Thank you. Has anyone else ever worn this rosary besides you?

FATHER: Not since my parents gave it to me. No.

GUSTAVITO: So it's just you and me. Who do you confess to?

FATHER: I go to another church. A priest in another parish.

GUSTAVITO: I thought for a second you were gonna tell me you don't sin. Do priests have a club?

FATHER: No. Maybe you should give me back my rosary now.

GUSTAVITO: Still, if you walk down the street you can always spot each other. That's kinda neat, isn't it? *(He studies the rosary.)* It's beautiful.

FATHER: You're a good boy, Gustavito.

GUSTAVITO: Everybody says so. Can I say one prayer with it on?

FATHER: All right.

(GUSTAVITO prays silently. He crosses himself and removes the rosary.)

GUSTAVITO: Mercy makes promises. She makes a bargain with God and if she gets what she wants she'll do a novena or a week of rosaries. Does that work?

FATHER: Sometimes God listens. Sometimes He'll take pity.

GUSTAVITO: Can I put the rosary back on you?

(FATHER bends over slightly. GUSTAVITO, who is kneeling, cannot reach him.)

GUSTAVITO: You have to kneel.

FATHER: No, you stand.

GUSTAVITO: This is a holy ritual. You gotta kneel for these things.

(FATHER kneels. GUSTAVITO is placing the rosary around the FATHER's neck, who places his hands on GUSTAVITO's hands to guide them.)

GUSTAVITO: Maybe I can confess you. I can be a priest trainee.

(FATHER stands.)

GUSTAVITO: But you probably don't have that many sins. Not like me. And I don't even remember sinning that much.

FATHER: Gustavito, when you come to visit me, let's just keep it a secret, okay? Just between us two.

GUSTAVITO: Like best friends?

FATHER: Like best friends.

(JUNIOR *is smoking on the fire escape.* GUSTAVITO *enters the fire escape carrying two glasses of Tang. In the living room we can see the sewing dummy with a semi-fabulous wedding dress on it. Every time we see the wedding dress it has become more and more elaborate.* NORRY *and* MERCY *fuss around the dummy.* NORRY *has brought a large sequined spider that he moves from place to place on the dress. After every new placement he will take a few steps back and turn away from the dress only to spin around again quickly to get the full "surprise" effect of the newest location.*)

JUNIOR: Took you long enough.

GUSTAVITO: You wanted me to add sugar, right?

JUNIOR: Don't give me lip `cause I'll throw you the fuck offa here.

(GUSTAVITO *sits, sipping his drink.*)

GUSTAVITO: I hope it don't rain.

JUNIOR: If it does we just wait right here. I ain't going in there while the freak is there. It's not even supposed to be here while we're here. (*He looks down.*) Oh shit man, there's Zoraya. Hey, Zoraya. (*He makes kissing noises.*) Hey, baby, don't be acting so fucking stuck up. It's too late for that. I had you.

GUSTAVITO: She don't like you.

(JUNIOR *hits him, hard.*)

JUNIOR: If you cry and get Mercy out here I'll crack your head.

(GUSTAVITO *cries quietly.*)

(*Inside*)

NORRY: I've tried to convince myself, but honey this spider ain't working.

MERCY: Who ever heard of a spider on a wedding dress?

NORRY: This dress is never gonna be finished.

MERCY: Forever in the making.

NORRY: It has to be special.

MERCY: Trust me, on you it'll be special.

NORRY: Did you wear white?

MERCY: Fresh.

NORRY: So sensitive.

MERCY: I can still wear white. I'm kidding.

NORRY: I don't think you are.

MERCY: And you're right. It's none of your business.

NORRY: Doctor Norry is in. How to get a man? Honey hush, you've come to the right place. 'Cause there's a right way and a wrong way and the wrong way just sends them running. Trust me, I know.

MERCY: Hand me the scissors.

(NORRY *does.* MERCY *very carefully snips away stray threads as* NORRY *speaks.*)

NORRY: How to keep a man? Ooooh, you've got to keep him interested.

(GUSTAVITO *leans in to listen.*)

NORRY: Find out what his fantasies are. Find the ones he doesn't even know about himself. If you can do that, you'll own him. Lust has a very short leash. How to get rid of a man? Kill him.

(MERCY *laughs.*)

MERCY: Ave Maria, Norry.

NORRY: No, I'm serious. Men don't understand from goodbye unless they're the ones saying it.

(*Fire escape*)

GUSTAVITO: What's a fantasy?

(JUNIOR *takes out another cigarette.*)

JUNIOR: It's what I am to Zoraya. She just be dreaming about me day and night. (*He bangs on the window.*) Hey, let's wrap it up in there.

GUSTAVITO: Junior, teach me how to smoke.

(JUNIOR *hands him the lit cigarette from his own mouth.*)

JUNIOR: Knock yourself out. (*He lights another one for himself.*) No, breathe in through your mouth and out through your nose. Like this. (*He demonstrates.*)

GUSTAVITO: Did Kiko teach you how to smoke?

JUNIOR: Man, Kiko wouldn't know how to shit if Mercy didn't tell him how. He is totally pussy whipped by her. I don't have any respect for him. Love fucks you up. It's true.

GUSTAVITO: Zoraya went in her house.

JUNIOR: I ain't blind. I saw it.

MERCY: Once a year I get violets. A little bouquet in the fall. I never know who sends them. "Secret Admirer".

NORRY: Yeah?

MERCY: For a week after I get them Kiko is very nice to me.

NORRY: I'm surprised he doesn't throw them out.

MERCY: He wouldn't dare. I'd kill him. They're mine. The only thing in this house that's mine. Third wife.

NORRY: What happened to the other two?

MERCY: Consuelo died and Esperanza just up and disappeared. I still think she's gonna walk in someday and take back everything.

NORRY: He'd be a fool to give up somebody as special as you. I gotta go. Don Kiko should be home soon. (*He collects his things.*)

MERCY: See you tomorrow?

NORRY: Like always. You want to come to the club sometime?

MERCY: You always ask.

NORRY: Well, you always tell me no.

MERCY: I can't.

NORRY: Someday we'll do a number together, okay?

(MERCY *and* NORRY *kiss each other on the cheek. He exits. She goes to the window.*)

MERCY: You can come in now.

JUNIOR: Not until you fumigate.

(GUSTAVITO *enters living room.*)

GUSTAVITO: Be nice to Junior, he got love trouble.

(JUNIOR *enters and smacks* GUSTAVITO, *who in turn hits him back.*)

GUSTAVITO: I didn't say nothing.

JUNIOR: It's that nothing that's gonna get you killed.

(MERCY *hits* JUNIOR *while trying to keep* GUSTAVITO *and* JUNIOR *apart.*)

GUSTAVITO: Like it's my fault Zoraya thinks you're stupid.

(In this exchange of smacks, KIKO enters. He is drunk and embraces MERCY from behind and tries to kiss her.)

MERCY: Get the hell off me.

KIKO: Come on, Mercedita, just one little kiss.

(MERCY pushes him off.)

MERCY: Oh, fuck, now I gotta get my hammer.

(MERCY exits into the kitchen. KIKO follows her. Their arguing voices are heard by JUNIOR and GUSTAVITO. GUSTAVITO puts his hands on his ears and tries to sing loudly to drown out the argument. JUNIOR takes his pack of cigarettes and throws it to GUSTAVITO. JUNIOR motions him to be quiet.)

JUNIOR: Sssh. Just don't set this dump on fire.

(The arguing slowly fades as JUNIOR exits. GUSTAVITO puts a cigarette to his lips and strikes a match. Lights fade except on match. GUSTAVITO lights his cigarette. Lights come up on GUSTAVITO smoking in the rectory. Enter FATHER.)

FATHER: Put out that cigarette.

GUSTAVITO: No.

(FATHER takes the cigarette out of GUSTAVITO's mouth. GUSTAVITO flinches.)

FATHER: You can't go home smelling of cigarettes.

(FATHER begins smoking the cigarette.)

GUSTAVITO: Hey, that's mine.

FATHER: That's mine, what?

GUSTAVITO: That's mine, Father.

(FATHER sits, and continues to smoke cigarette.)

FATHER: Is it yours?

(GUSTAVITO nods.)

FATHER: If it's yours, come get it.

(GUSTAVITO *slowly approaches* FATHER.)

FATHER: I shouldn't be smoking it if it's yours. It is yours, isn't it?

(GUSTAVITO *nods; he is now standing next to* FATHER.)

FATHER: Take it from me.

(GUSTAVITO *reaches for the cigarette.*)

FATHER: Slowly.

(GUSTAVITO *moves slowly.*)

FATHER: You know, we can both smoke it. We can share.

(GUSTAVITO *hesitates.*)

FATHER: There won't be much cigarette left. Take it from my mouth.

(GUSTAVITO *moves to do so.*)

FATHER: Gently.

(GUSTAVITO *does.* FATHER *exhales.*)

FATHER: Now put it in yours.

(GUSTAVITO *does.*)

FATHER: Smoke.

(GUSTAVITO *does.*)

FATHER: Inhale deeply.

(GUSTAVITO *does and coughs.*)

FATHER: Put it back in my mouth.

(GUSTAVITO *does.*)

FATHER: Hold it close to me. So that my lips can reach out and touch it. Where did you get the cigarettes? Your hand is shaking. Stop it. Bring it closer to my lips.

(GUSTAVITO *does.*)

FATHER: You stole them, didn't you?

GUSTAVITO: Yes, Father.

FATHER: Put it in my mouth.

(He inhales deeply.)

FATHER: Cigarettes are bad for you.

GUSTAVITO: Yes, father.

FATHER: And so is stealing. Hold it away from me. Did you steal anything else while you were waiting for me?

GUSTAVITO: No, father. I would never do that.

FATHER: How do I know? Smoke, please.

(GUSTAVITO puts it to FATHER's lips.)

FATHER: How do I know what a common thief would do? Hold it away from me.

GUSTAVITO: I'm going to burn myself, Father.

FATHER: Yes, you just might. Keep holding it.

(The cigarette is dangerously near the end. GUSTAVITO winces in pain.)

FATHER: If you drop it I will burn for your sins.

(GUSTAVITO begins to shake.)

FATHER: You lie, you steal. Why are you so bad?

(GUSTAVITO is crying now.)

GUSTAVITO: I don't know, Father.

FATHER: Put the cigarette down.

(GUSTAVITO does. FATHER blows on GUSTAVITO's fingers.)

FATHER: They're not burnt at all.

(GUSTAVITO begins to blow on the FATHER's fingers.)

FATHER: Why don't you go home? Please. I am not the proper friend for you. If you come back I'll have to go. Please don't do this to me.

(GUSTAVITO *exits. A subway car.* NORRY *is standing; enter* GUSTAVITO.)

TOUGH: *(V/O)* Any faggots on this train? I want all faggots off this train.

(NORRY *grabs* GUSTAVITO *by the back of the neck and kisses him full on the mouth.*)

NORRY: What was that? You wanted to help all faggots get off on this train? Don't worry about me, hon, I'm doing okay on my own. But, any straight boys who have never lusted after other boys on this train? That's a much more interesting question. Let's see a show of hands. And don't lie. I know who you are. Just look me in the eye and say it. This is our stop.

(NORRY *taps* GUSTAVITO *on the shoulder.*)

GUSTAVITO: I...

NORRY: You want to stay on this train by yourself?

(NORRY *gets off the subway.* GUSTAVITO *hurriedly follows him.*)

GUSTAVITO: You could have gotten us killed.

NORRY: They'd have to stop blushing first. Pendejo boys. No cojones kids on that train, honey. All they can do is beat you up.

GUSTAVITO: Kill you.

NORRY: Okay, so kill you, big deal. I was in high heels and I was chased by a bunch of these guys. They caught me and beat the shit out of me. I didn't hang up my heels. I just made them higher. I am a kamikaze queer. My first boyfriend was an inflatable doll. I think his name was Scott. You're a little far from home. This is my neck of the woods. Give you a tour?

GUSTAVITO: Of what?

NORRY: Paradise. How old are you again?

GUSTAVITO: Thirteen.

NORRY: So which is it? Twelve or God forbid, eleven? *(Silence)* Don't tell me ten. It's a good thing I woke up feeling motherly. I'll show you around, but be careful. The streets are hungry for cute boys.

GUSTAVITO: I'm not cute.

NORRY: No, you're not. But with my help you could be. I'm bringing you into a bar.

GUSTAVITO: They won't let me in.

NORRY: Oh, so you've tried already. I don't think you're ready yet, but just so you can see that you're not missing a whole lot. Knew you were gay the second I laid eyes on you.

GUSTAVITO: Huh?

NORRY: Now when we enter, own it. Let all the eyes hit you at once.

GUSTAVITO: They'll knock me off my feet.

NORRY: How can they, baby, if you don't give a shit? *(Before they enter he stifles a theatrical yawn.)* Lead with the attitude.

(NORRY *walks in, followed by* GUSTAVITO.)

NORRY: Let them take you in. Chill, bitch. This race is in slow mo.

(GUSTAVITO *nervously looks around.*)

NORRY: You better look cool or you'll answer to me. Raise your eyes slowly. Make eye contact. Lock into position. Now break. Break! You have to do it before they do. You have to win. Close your mouth, dear. We're window dressing, not window shopping.

GUSTAVITO: I can't breathe.

NORRY: Breathing's overrated. But if you must breathe do it so it makes you look like the hottest person in the world. Touch the back of your neck.

GUSTAVITO: What?

NORRY: Right hand, slowly on the nape.

(GUSTAVITO *does.*)

NORRY: Now turn, just the head.

GUSTAVITO: Left? Right?

NORRY: Left. Make that eye contact.

(GUSTAVITO *does.*)

GUSTAVITO: Who? Oh.

NORRY: One down. Sixty-nine to go.

(GUSTAVITO *bites his lower lip.*)

NORRY: Oooh. Self taught?

GUSTAVITO: What?

NORRY: And coy.

GUSTAVITO: That guy smirked at me.

NORRY: Sure, `cause he can't have you. The bottom line is you never lose. Gustavito, never let yourself lose. Do you wanna dance?

GUSTAVITO: I'm not ready. Don't do this to me.

NORRY: What am I doing? *(Playfully)* What am I doing?

GUSTAVITO: I don't know how to do this.

NORRY: Ah, so pure. So innocent. Let me explain it to you so you can understand it. *(Screams)* You like dick!

(GUSTAVITO *disappears into his hands.* NORRY *points at him and speaks to the crowd.*)

NORRY: Right here, right now, my buddy boy here likes men. He likes all men. Sweaty men, clean men, dirty men. Tall, good-looking men and the men that might

not grab your attention at first sight but know enough
to call a trick by their rightful name. Old men, young
men. No, I don't think younger would be physically
possible. But he's flexible. He's poised and he can be
yours for the low low price of a drink and a smile. He'd
prefer someone nice but is willing to negotiate. (*Returns
his attention to* GUSTAVITO) That was cruel, wasn't it?

GUSTAVITO: Yes.

NORRY: It's a gift.

(GUSTAVITO *begins to cry on the bar.*)

NORRY: Hey, hey. I'm sorry. Wait a second. It's a man,
isn't it?

(GUSTAVITO *nods.*)

NORRY: The man has not been born who is worth one
of your tears.

(GUSTAVITO *cries louder.*)

NORRY: Louder doesn't mean you love him any more.
Now shut up.

(GUSTAVITO *does.*)

GUSTAVITO: I want money for the jukebox.

NORRY: So you can put on some sorry-ass "my man
just left me" song? I don't think so.

GUSTAVITO: He doesn't love me.

NORRY: My God, a drama queen at your age.

GUSTAVITO: He doesn't.

NORRY: Do you even know what love is?

(GUSTAVITO *gives him a dirty look.*)

NORRY: Hey, for heartbreak to exist the heart has got
to be in some real danger. Imaginary lover, imaginary
heartbreak. It's a rule. Don't go breaking rules on me,
honey.

(The living room. MERCY has fallen asleep attaching seed pearls to NORRY's wedding dress. She has aimed a desk lamp to the folds of the skirt and pulled up a chair upon which she now sleeps. The only light in the room is from the desk lamp. KIKO enters. He turns on the light and turns it off quickly after seeing that MERCY is asleep. He gently walks up to her, but does not touch her.)

KIKO: You're gonna go blind. *(She does not stir. He looks at the wedding dress in admiration.)* You have an art, my Mercedes. *(He studies her.)* It should have been you. First and for always.

(He tries to pick her up; she whispers in her sleep.)

MERCY: Norry.

(KIKO rises and exits.)

(Later, GUSTAVITO is waiting for JUNIOR on the front steps.)

GUSTAVITO: Hey, Junior.

JUNIOR: Hey, stupid. *(He is about to enter their building.)*

GUSTAVITO: Don't go up there. Zoraya's up there. She's talking to Kiko.

JUNIOR: About what?

GUSTAVITO: About you and shit and how you won't leave her alone.

JUNIOR: That's bullshit.

GUSTAVITO: She's got Kiko all worked up. She said she don't want nothing to do with you.

JUNIOR: Oh yeah? Let her tell me to my face. *(He again is about to enter the building.)*

GUSTAVITO: Kiko's gonna make you apologize to her.

(JUNIOR stops.)

GUSTAVITO: He's got his belt around his shoulders and after you apologize he's gonna beat you right in front of her. Zoraya said she don't like you and she never gave you—

JUNIOR: She's lying.

GUSTAVITO: —any indication that she was—

JUNIOR: That is such fucking bullshit.

GUSTAVITO: —interested or nothing. Her father's upstairs, too.

(JUNIOR *is defeated.*)

JUNIOR: She's gonna have my baby.

GUSTAVITO: When?

JUNIOR: Someday.

GUSTAVITO: Did she ever like you?

JUNIOR: She was fucking crazy about me. In school, she was like the one who would follow me in the hallways. See? This is woman, Gustavito. My mother dies, your mother leaves, and Mercy's like counting the goddamn days until she's outta here. Women leave. That's it. You treat them right, you treat them wrong, they leave.

GUSTAVITO: Mercy's not going no place.

JUNIOR: You wait and see.

(GUSTAVITO *digs into his pocket and gives* JUNIOR *some money.*)

GUSTAVITO: I took this from Kiko's wallet. Go to the Fairmont and see a double feature. Zoraya will be gone by then.

(JUNIOR *takes the money.*)

JUNIOR: I love her, you know? You tell me what I'm doing wrong, 'cause I don't see it. She's supposed to be mine.

GUSTAVITO: Junior, maybe I'm in love, too.

JUNIOR: You better not be. *(He exits.)*

GUSTAVITO: Please don't ruin it for me.

(It begins to rain. The FATHER's *living quarters.* GUSTAVITO *enters; he is obviously quite drunk.)*

GUSTAVITO: Father?

*(*FATHER *enters. They stare at each other.)*

GUSTAVITO: Hi.

FATHER: Go home.

GUSTAVITO: *(Laughs)* I'm all wet.

FATHER: Don't you have an umbrella?

GUSTAVITO: I lost it. I didn't want to tell Kiko. Umbrellas cost money, you know.

*(*FATHER *exits offstage.)*

FATHER: Wait right there. Don't move around a lot. Take off your shoes.

GUSTAVITO: I was walking, that's where I was. I stole a bottle of Don Q from Kiko so I'm a little bit a lot of lit. But that's okay cause that the only way sometimes you can talk, right? The rain tastes pretty good. If you lean back you can get it in your mouth. Just keep your eyes closed.

*(*FATHER *enters with towel.)*

FATHER: You didn't take off your shoes.

GUSTAVITO: You told me not to move.

FATHER: Take off your jacket and your shoes.

*(*GUSTAVITO *removes his jacket.)*

FATHER: Give it to me.

*(*FATHER *takes the jacket and spreads it out on the altar railing.* GUSTAVITO *is having trouble untying his laces.)*

GUSTAVITO: I can't get the knot untied. They're wet.

FATHER: Hold on. *(He gets on his hands and knees and tries to untie the laces.)* Why do you knot them?

GUSTAVITO: I'm sorry. *(He looks down at the* FATHER *and laughs.)* I do this for Kiko.

FATHER: Is he your father?

GUSTAVITO: Yeah.

FATHER: Then call him your father.

GUSTAVITO: Then what do I call you?

*(*FATHER *removes one sneaker.)*

FATHER: You can untie the other one.

*(*GUSTAVITO *sits on the floor and removes his other sneaker.* FATHER *crouches behind him and dries his hair.* GUSTAVITO *begins to pray.)*

GUSTAVITO: Every time I make a mistake I have to start again. Sometimes a whole day goes by and I can only say one prayer right. I start thinking about other things. *(He looks away from* FATHER.*)* I love you.

FATHER: Don't say that.

GUSTAVITO: I walked around a lot all night trying to talk myself out of it, but it's not happening. No no no no no. *(Holds on to the chair. Steadies himself.)* To your face. Drunk? I'm not that drunk. I will remember this. You hear me?

FATHER: Yeah.

GUSTAVITO: `Cause you're all quiet, so...make me nervous. Do we kiss now?

FATHER: No.

*(*GUSTAVITO *slides down the chair. He is now kneeling.)*

FATHER: You have to go home.

GUSTAVITO: Hey hey.

(FATHER *goes to* GUSTAVITO *and tries to help him stand.*
GUSTAVITO *tries to kiss him.* FATHER *turns his head.*)

FATHER: Come on, sit down.

GUSTAVITO: You sit and I'll sit on your lap.

(FATHER *lowers* GUSTAVITO *onto the chair. He kisses*
GUSTAVITO's *hair.*)

GUSTAVITO: We'll go someplace where I'm not stupid
and you're not a priest.

(*A knock is heard.*)

FATHER: Get back in the chair.

GUSTAVITO: That's my brother and I'm a gonna kick his
ass. That's—

FATHER: Be quiet.

GUSTAVITO: —who it is, you know.

FATHER: Sssh.

GUSTAVITO: I'm afraid—

(*More knocks on door*)

JUNIOR: (*Voice only*) I can get real loud out here.

GUSTAVITO: —if I close my eyes I'm gonna drown.

(GUSTAVITO *leans against* FATHER *and collapses.* FATHER
carries him to the bed and lays him down.)

JUNIOR: (*Voice only*) Don't try to hide behind stained
glass.

(FATHER *opens the door.*)

FATHER: Is there something I can do for you?

JUNIOR: Fuck you. I just want my brother.

FATHER: He's not here.

JUNIOR: I have a hard time believing that. Maybe I
should just call the cops so they can look.

FATHER: There's a pay phone on the corner. *(Pause)*

JUNIOR: He comes by you send him home.

FATHER: Why?

(JUNIOR punches FATHER in the stomach, who crouches in pain.)

JUNIOR: My hand slipped. Stupid questions do that to me.

(FATHER is about to step outside but he hears GUSTAVITO moving on the bed. GUSTAVITO has gone under the covers and removed his shirt. He throws it at FATHER's feet. JUNIOR does not see it, and FATHER slowly inches it away by using his foot.)

FATHER: If you don't leave right now I'll be the one calling the police.

JUNIOR: Home. The second you see him.

(JUNIOR exits. FATHER turns to see GUSTAVITO sleeping on his bed. FATHER holds the tee shirt in front of himself and looks in the mirror. He sees his reflection and also sees GUSTAVITO sleeping. He goes to the bed and stands by it. GUSTAVITO takes his hand.)

GUSTAVITO: Thank you. If I couldn't see you anymore I would kill myself.

FATHER: No, you wouldn't.

GUSTAVITO: I love you more than anybody else.

FATHER: Go to sleep.

GUSTAVITO: My head is spinning.

FATHER: You'll be fine.

GUSTAVITO: Tell me you love me. And tell me we can be together.

FATHER: No, we can't.

(GUSTAVITO struggles to sit up. He puts his arms around FATHER's neck and closes his eyes.)

GUSTAVITO: I'm safe. I'm not going.

(FATHER's arms slowly embrace GUSTAVITO.)

GUSTAVITO: I love coming to church to hear you talk to God. Sometimes I imagine it's just you, me, and God. And He listens to you, you know, `cause you like know all this stuff. And I feel stupid proud just watching you...I would kill myself.

(GUSTAVITO tries to kiss FATHER on the lips; FATHER moves away.)

FATHER: When you imagine that it's just you, me, and God, does God ever say anything?

(GUSTAVITO has fallen asleep.)

FATHER: I need to know if He talks to you, because He doesn't talk to me.

(FATHER puts GUSTAVITO back on the bed. He exits to the church area and kneels before the cross.)

FATHER: I'm going to lose this war.

(The living room. NORRY is wearing a showgirl outfit and standing by the wedding dress. He sings simply and sweetly.)

NORRY: *(Sings)* I've locked my heart
I'll keep my feelings there
Said I've stocked my heart
With icy frigid air
And I mean to care for no one
Because I'm through with love

I'm through with love
Won't ever fall again
Said adieu to love
Don't ever call again

For I must have you or no one
And so I'm through with love

(MERCY *applauds while* JUNIOR *joins in, sarcastically.*)

JUNIOR: *Adios, loca.*

(NORRY *grabs his crotch in a response.* JUNIOR *calls out the window.*)

JUNIOR: Gustavito!

MERCY: He's in church.

JUNIOR: No, he's not.

MERCY: Yes, he is.

JUNIOR: It's eight at night.

MERCY: So? The priest will bring him home.

JUNIOR: ...Yeah, okay. *(He exits.)*

NORRY: You know, every time I see one of those *Bride* magazines I get all confused. White? Off white? Cream? Chartreuse?

(MERCY *studies* NORRY.)

MERCY: No matter what I would do to myself I could never look as beautiful as you do now.

NORRY: Mercedes.

MERCY: The miracle maker. *La milagrosa.*

(NORRY *stands behind the dummy. It's almost as if he's wearing the wedding dress.*)

NORRY: What do you think?

(MERCY *smooths out the skirt.*)

MERCY: I'm afraid of the day it'll be finished.

NORRY: I can chart our history on this dress. When we had fights, when we made up. When we did each other's hair.

(MERCY *begins to adjust the bodice.*)

(GUSTAVITO *rises and enters the church area, where he kneels, lights a candle, and begins to pray. Behind the church where* FATHER *has parked his car,* JUNIOR *enters with a tire iron.)*

JUNIOR: You know, Padre, I warned you about leaving your car just anywhere. Nothing is safe anymore.

(JUNIOR *brings the tire iron crashing down on the* FATHER's *car.* GUSTAVITO *is lighting another votive candle. The lit candles surrounding him illustrate how long he has been at it.* JUNIOR *continues trashing* FATHER's *car. Image wise, it's almost as if* JUNIOR's *rage is making him pure. The sound of the car being destroyed is slowly replaced by a hymn. The sound increases as the demolition of the car increases.)*

(GUSTAVITO *continues his ritual—each candle, each prayer more impassioned than the last.)*

(JUNIOR *is circling the car, searching for something else to destroy. He kicks in the front passenger window and tries to do the same with the rear window. Glass enters his shoe. He screams, but cannot be heard above the hymn. The volume begins to decrease.* JUNIOR *limps and exits.)*

(MERCY *touches the dummy's breasts.* NORRY *and* MERCY *are both frozen, staring at each other.)*

NORRY: I don't trust straight people. *(He runs to the door.)*

MERCY: That door only works one way. You can't come back in.

(NORRY *turns from the door. He takes off an earring and throws it at* MERCY. *She doesn't respond. He takes off his other one and throws it at her. She catches it and puts it on her ear.)*

(KIKO *is on the street. He has bought a bouquet of violets. He exits.)*

(The church candle lights come up as the FATHER*'s car fades.* GUSTAVITO *is kneeling in prayer. Enter* FATHER, *carrying* GUSTAVITO*'s tee shirt. He stands, watching* GUSTAVITO, *and begins to pray.)*

GUSTAVITO: Excuse me, I was praying here.

FATHER: What are you praying for?

GUSTAVITO: I don't know.

FATHER: How can God grant your request if He doesn't know what it is?

GUSTAVITO: He knows. It's just me that don't know.

FATHER: That's a lot of candles. You must want something very badly.

GUSTAVITO: *(Correcting him)* Very much. I want something very much.

FATHER: But you don't know what it is.

GUSTAVITO: I'm not allowed to know....Father?

FATHER: Yes?

GUSTAVITO: Nothing. I want to wake up tomorrow and be you. That's what I want.

FATHER: I'm a thirty-year-old man, Gustavito, you're a ten-year-old boy. What you want is impossible. I'm not going to betray my life for you.

*(*FATHER *is about to exit, but stops to watch* GUSTAVITO, *who continues to pray.)*

GUSTAVITO: God?

MERCY: *(To* NORRY*)* Doesn't passion go where you live, either?

*(*NORRY *approaches* MERCY. *He unbuttons her house dress; she unzips his dress and slides it down to his waist.* NORRY *stares at* MERCY.*)*

NORRY: No matter what I would do to myself I could never look as beautiful as you do now.

(NORRY *holds up his hand but cannot bring himself to touch* MERCY. *She takes his hand and kisses it.*)

MERCY: Tell me I'm the first.

(NORRY *nods.* MERCY *gently puts his hand on her breast.*)

(JUNIOR *bursts in on* NORRY *and* MERCY. *His foot is bleeding and he leaves a trail of blood wherever he walks.* NORRY *and* MERCY *separate, but remain in partial undress.* JUNIOR *reels back as if struck.*)

JUNIOR: I'm not here. I'm not seeing this. Go someplace, Junior. Go someplace else.

(MERCY *and* NORRY *quickly put their clothes back on.*)

MERCY: Junior, wait a second.

JUNIOR: I'm not here. I'm not here. (*Slaps himself*) I'm not here. I'm not here. (*He points to* MERCY.)

JUNIOR: You. (*He begins to cry.*) Man, you like my mother. (*He begins to hit his head.*) But it's okay. It's okay. You can get the fuck out, too.

MERCY: Your foot. (*She tries to help him; he pushes her against the dummy.*)

JUNIOR: No, I'm okay. And when Kiko gets back, he'll take care of you. See, `cause I was in church. I know what the priest is up to and I found Kiko so now he knows, too.

MERCY: Norry, get out of here.

JUNIOR: Oh, the freak's got plenty of time. First Kiko's gotta kill the priest and then he can come back and kill the both of you.

NORRY: And Gustavito?

(MERCY *runs out of the apartment.* NORRY *tries to follow but* JUNIOR *blocks the door.*)

JUNIOR: You wait here for Kiko, mother fucker.

(JUNIOR *punches* NORRY. NORRY *stomps on his bleeding foot.* JUNIOR *screams and falls on the floor. He writhes in pain.*)

JUNIOR: Everybody's gonna die. He's gonna kill everybody.

(NORRY *crouches next to* JUNIOR.)

NORRY: I'm sorry.

JUNIOR: Now, you're scared, huh, mother fucker.

(NORRY *sits on the floor by* JUNIOR *and takes his foot in his lap.*)

JUNIOR: What you doing?

NORRY: Just gotta take off this shoe.

JUNIOR: Man, when Kiko come back he's gonna kill you. I'm a tell him everything.

NORRY: Honey, you don't know everything.

(NORRY *takes off* JUNIOR's *shoe.*)

JUNIOR: I think I'm gonna bleed to death.

(NORRY *shudders at seeing the bleeding foot. He very gently takes off the sock.*)

NORRY: No, you won't.

JUNIOR: You're gonna get blood all over you.

NORRY: I've had blood on me before. Been there. Done that. Packed a lunch. (*He reaches over to the sewing kit. He pulls out some tweezers.*)

JUNIOR: Whatta you gonna do?

NORRY: Pull out these glass splinters, stupid.

JUNIOR: If Kiko don't kill you, I will. I can't look.

NORRY: Look at the wall and tell me how you're gonna kill me.

(JUNIOR *looks away.* NORRY *starts to pull the glass splinters from his foot.* JUNIOR *grimaces in pain. He involuntarily grabs* NORRY's *shoulder.* NORRY *rips pieces off the wedding dress and sops up the blood. He does not look up from his task.*)

NORRY: You're so much easier to be nice to when I don't have to look at you.

(*Church.* MERCY's *voice calling out to* KIKO *is heard as if from very far away.* GUSTAVITO *rises. When he turns he sees the* FATHER.)

MERCY: *(Voice only)* Kiko! Kiko!

FATHER: Does He talk to you, because He doesn't talk to me.

GUSTAVITO: Nothing happens that God doesn't know about.

(GUSTAVITO *gently touches the* FATHER's *face. Very slowly, they kiss.*)

KIKO: *(Voice only)* Gustavito!

END OF ACT ONE

ACT TWO

(At Rise. The white, glowing cross appears. The Delgado family appears from behind it. They each carry a suitcase. They place their suit cases down and tilt the cross to the right. Airplane noise is heard. The cross has become an airplane. They make a small circle with it before returning it to its starting place.)

VOICE: Good morning. Now arriving at Gate 24 is American Airlines Flight 989 from New York. Welcome to Puerto Rico.

GUSTAVITO: Kiko told me he would kill the Father if I didn't come to Puerto Rico.

MERCY: Kiko told me he would kill Gustavito if I didn't come to Puerto Rico.

JUNIOR: Kiko told he would kill me if I didn't come to Puerto Rico.

KIKO: Their lips were touching. I don't know a lot but I know right from wrong. I know a sin when I see it.

(Lights up on the confessional. NORRY enters the penitent's side. Silence)

NORRY: Is it my line?

FATHER: Forgive me Father for I have sinned.

NORRY: Okay. Forgive me Father for I have sinned.

FATHER: How long has it been since your last confession?

(Silence. NORRY *earnestly tries to calculate the time.)*

FATHER: Why are you here?

NORRY: When you took the vow, you knew you were giving up a whole lot, right? But you did it `cause you had to. `Cause the call was so strong you had to. It was like destiny, you know what I'm saying?

FATHER: In the least.

NORRY: No? I thought if anybody would know about denial it would be you. I confess, Father. *(Pause)* You are my last recourse. Trust me, the words Catholic and comfort don't go hand in hand in my brain. Okay, my sin. For the last three years I have dreamt of this woman. Going against everything I am. Everything I am happy to be.

FATHER: The problem is she's...?

NORRY: The problem is she's a she. The problem is I'm going to have to change who I am to love this person. The problem is we're not even the same size. I used to dream of being accepted, so I found a world, a small world, where I could be. Where if I follow the rules I could be accepted. But, I never stopped resenting the rights other people took for granted. The gentle kiss, the hand holding in public, the "Hello, we're a couple, we fuck, and how are you?" that men and women take for granted. Bitter? I left bitter in the dust. I see families, "traditional families", and I get teary-eyed even as I laugh at them. Aren't they just the stupidest thing? Hello? Are you still there? Hello?

FATHER: I'm here.

NORRY: Feel free to interrupt me at any time with those pearls of wisdom that are just dying to leave your lips.

FATHER: Let's leave my lips out of this.

NORRY: Done. I am happy to be who I am. I am proud to be who I am. So why can't I forget her? *(Pause)* Father, I think you know what I'm talking about. Can you broker a deal with God for me?

FATHER: I don't do that.

NORRY: If your God, *the* God, any God can take her away from my heart after these three years I will give them my plumage. Just give me peace...and give her happiness. That's it. That's my prayer.

(FATHER leaves the confessional. Pause. NORRY approaches him. He takes off his wig and drops to one knee, takes the FATHER's hand, and kisses it.)

NORRY: This. Will take. Some getting used to.

(NORRY exits. FATHER looks at his kissed hand. He crosses himself with it.)

FATHER: Three years. Amateur.

(NORRY and MERCY from Puerto Rico and New York)

MERCY & NORRY: I don't even know where to look. She's forgotten all about me by now.

MERCY: I mean he. He's forgotten all about me.

NORRY: Packed up and left in the night.

MERCY: I dream of you.

NORRY: *Bon voyage.*

MERCY: Kiko would have killed you.

NORRY: Forget me.

MERCY: You're a tattoo on my memory.

NORRY: Stop that.

MERCY: You're the sheet I cover myself with at night.

NORRY: Would I still be beautiful to you now?

(FATHER and KIKO, from Puerto Rico and New York)

FATHER & KIKO: I am not a bad man.

KIKO: My family is sacred to me. As his God should be to him. I have a right to defend what's mine. I will not let my son drown.

(MERCY *kneels. She is clothed in a white "habit" dress and wears a green belt made of yarn. She looks very plain except for the earring that she wears, the earring that* NORRY *threw at her.*)

MERCY: Dear God, let's make a deal.

FATHER: Gustavito, your father loves you very much.

KIKO: Someday Gustavito will put his arm around me and thank me. Someday he will say, "Thank you, Kiko, for saving me."

FATHER: What did one father say to the other father?

KIKO: I would make an empty space where that kiss had lived. You have to understand—

FATHER & KIKO: I am not a bad man.

FATHER: What did one father say to the other father?

KIKO: My son is telling me he loves him.

FATHER: What did one father say to the other father? Why did you take my son from me?

KIKO: Why did you take my son?

(GUSTAVITO *and* JUNIOR *in Puerto Rico.* GUSTAVITO *lights up a cigarette.*)

GUSTAVITO: I don't know when I'm going but I'm going.

JUNIOR: It's your fault we're here.

(*Pause.* GUSTAVITO *and* JUNIOR *stare at each other.*)

JUNIOR: Accept it, deal with it, grow from it.

(GUSTAVITO *and* JUNIOR *share the cigarette back and forth. They smoke in silence.*)

JUNIOR: Of all the people in the world to be nice to me why did it have to be him? He tore a piece off that wedding dress that mattered so much to him, for me. He did that for me.

(GUSTAVITO *puts his head in his hands.*)

JUNIOR: Gustavito.

GUSTAVITO: Sssh. I'm trying to send a message.

(*After a few beats* JUNIOR *assumes* GUSTAVITO's *position and also tries to send a message.*)

FATHER: I think about him sometimes.

KIKO: He'll thank me someday.

FATHER: Sometimes.

(MERCY *crosses herself and rises.*)

MERCY: Don't forget about me, God.

GUSTAVITO: *(To God)* Please let me be angry. It's the only way I'll survive.

NORRY: My idea of an anatomically correct woman was always Barbie. Talk about your midlife crisis slash career change.

(KIKO *has his pants rolled up. He is in the "river" where he first saw* MERCY, *who enters carrying a mug of coffee and a towel.*)

MERCY: Hey, Mister, this is the Gomez River. You're on our property.

(KIKO *and* MERCY *laugh.*)

KIKO: And then did I fall or did you push me in?

MERCY: You fell, but I helped you out.

KIKO: Yeah, you took my hand. And then Consuelo came running up to me with a towel. Esperanza was *(looking on.)*

MERCY: *(Cutting him off)* Esperanza wasn't even home that day. I brought you some coffee. *(She hands it to him. He tries to take her hand; she slips it away.)*

KIKO: It's not the same island we left.

MERCY: Kiko, maybe we should go back. The boys aren't happy and you can get your old job back.

KIKO: No.

MERCY: Gustavito's eyes have died.

KIKO: Tell me, do you think my family respects me or fears me? *(Silence)* If anybody tries to leave I will kill them. You have my permission to tell them. I'm an ugly man.

MERCY: My mother used to say, "The uglier the man is the better."

KIKO: No, Mercy. I'm an ugly man. *(He blows on his coffee.)* If I throw this in your face, I would disfigure you. You would be ugly, too. You would never leave me.

MERCY: Drink your coffee.

KIKO: The water is nice and cool. You want to join me?

MERCY: I have no intention of joining you. Get out of there. You're gonna get sick and I'm not in the mood to take care of you.

(KIKO gets out of the water. MERCY goes to dry his feet but he stops her.)

KIKO: No, let Gustavito do it. *(He calls out.)* Gustavito! Gustavito! Gustavito! I guess Gustavito can't hear me.

MERCY: That must be it.

(KIKO takes the towel. He sits on the ground and dries his feet. He laughs at himself.)

KIKO: I can't sleep. I was ready to kill the Father but I would've had to have killed Gustavito, too. He

wouldn't let me hurt his priest, his Father. I make the
Father kneel. I make him beg my forgiveness and then
I start beating him. You try to pull me off, but nothing
can stop me. And then Gustavito's hands are hitting
me. He loves this man who is weeping on the floor.
And I grabbed Gustavito's lips. I was going to rip them
off, because I couldn't stand looking at them anymore,
and there was no fear in him. None. There's fear,
shame in the Father but none in the boy. So, why can't
I sleep? I keep seeing Gustavito without a mouth. *(He
runs his fingers gently over* MERCY's *mouth.)* A gaping
hole where that kissed had lived. Poof. No more kiss.

*(*FATHER *has finished Mass. He takes* GUSTAVITO's *baseball
cap from its hiding place and places it on the altar and talks
to it.)*

FATHER: Not a great Mass today. Attendance is down,
apathy is up. I think pizza for dinner would be good
tonight. What do you think? Maybe. You'll get married
someday to a very nice woman. Someone who will
love you very very much. And you'll have lots of
children. I think you will make a wonderful father.
And someday, way down the line, you'll come back
with your family and walk into my church and you'll
be happier than I ever could have made you. Maybe
you'll even forget all about me. God bless you. For
the first time in my life I'm afraid of dying. Of taking
all my secrets with me. With all that would be unsaid
and a God who never knew me. You were supposed to
show me the way. I can fake this. I have for years.

*(*GUSTAVITO *kneels. He takes the* FATHER's *rosary from his
pocket and places it around his neck.)*

GUSTAVITO: Por mi culpa, por mi culpa, por mi gran
culpa. I want to make You a promise, God, but I don't
know what You want.

*(*JUNIOR *enters the river site.)*

KIKO: You want to go in? The waters feel good.

JUNIOR: Nah.

KIKO: You know, let's get a couple of beers. Huh?
Okay? Okay. Maybe we can go play some dominoes.
I always said you were too young, but you're a man
now. You understand. You're not a boy anymore, you
know I did the right thing.

JUNIOR: ...Yeah.

KIKO: Mercy don't get it. You see the promise dress
she's wearing? She's made a promise to God. And
Saint Judas. That's what the green belt is for. Saint
Judas, the patron saint of impossible causes.

JUNIOR: She's just got a guilty conscience, that's all.

KIKO: She's made a promise with Saint Judas that I die
soon.

(FATHER, *in the confessional, lights a cigarette, smokes for a
few seconds, then holds it away from himself as* GUSTAVITO
did.)

NORRY: *(Sings)*
Jesus loves me this I know
For the Bible tells me so
Little ones to Him belong
They are weak but He is strong
(He stands behind the wedding dress.)
Well, technically, I'm not wearing it. Right, God? Uh,
God?

(JUNIOR *enters* MERCY *and* KIKO's *bedroom. From a trunk
he removes a glittery dress that* MERCY *had started, but
never finished, for* NORRY. *He stares at it.*)

JUNIOR: Fucking freak.

(*He moves the dress as if it were worn by someone. He sings,
very softly.*)

JUNIOR: I'm through with love
I'll never fall again
Said I'm through with love
(He is stumped momentarily for the words.)
La la la la la la
For I must have you or no one
And so I'm through with love

(MERCY enters.)

MERCY: We're gonna eat.

JUNIOR: Yeah, okay. *(He remains frozen in place.)*

MERCY: Now.

(JUNIOR throws the dress on the floor.)

MERCY: Go get your brother.

(JUNIOR exits. KIKO enters.)

MERCY: We're going to eat.

KIKO: Uh-huh. What's with you?

MERCY: Nothing.

KIKO: You want a kiss?

MERCY: No.

KIKO: Are you sure?

MERCY: I'm very sure.

(MERCY has turned away.)

KIKO: ...Do you want me dead? I'm not stupid, you
know.

MERCY: I know. You're the king of this house.

(JUNIOR enters.)

KIKO: Where's Gustavito?

JUNIOR: He's not hungry.

KIKO: Go get him.

JUNIOR: He's praying.

KIKO: In this house we eat when I say we eat. Serve the food. He's gonna eat. `Cause I want him to eat.

MERCY: Please don't do this, Kiko.

KIKO: `Cause I said he was going to eat.

(Lights down on family. Up on FATHER.*)*

FATHER: I was giving Mass the other day and my mind went blank. Just before we got to the Communion. Blank. I throw in a little Latin, bless the crowd a couple of times. No one noticed. And I thought to myself, "It finally happened. God is gone." I'm giving Communion and looking at the little wafers and I want to laugh, "This is supposed to feed your soul? You couldn't even make a good sandwich out of this." I'm the only one who sees this. They all believe. They all believe me as I bless them in the name of the Father, the Son, and the Holy Gustavito, amen. One after another they don't hear it. At my next Mass I will recite the twenty-third psalm, the psalm of Gustavito. They will not hear that, either. No, they won't.

(Lights up on the Delgado family at the dinner table. KIKO *walks* GUSTAVITO *to the table.* GUSTAVITO *is dressed older; his walk and manner are more in keeping with the teenage boy he is.* KIKO *places a plate of food in front of* GUSTAVITO, *who does not eat.* KIKO *becomes enraged and forces a handful of food into* GUSTAVITO's *mouth.* KIKO *and* JUNIOR *exit.* MERCY *tries to clean up a bit and then exits. She reenters with a bag of Oreos, and sits next to* GUSTAVITO *and begins to eat.)*

MERCY: Don't even ask for one `cause they're all mine. And they're so good. Look, Gustavito, Oreos.

*(*GUSTAVITO *continues to stare blankly ahead.)*

MERCY: You remember staying home when you were sick and I would give you Oreos for breakfast? I loved when you stayed home with me. All you had to do was sneeze and I would keep you out of school. You were such good company and you would help me sew. Well, look at this, I never noticed before but they look like chocolate Communion wafers, don't they? *(Silence)* Well, yes, Mercy, I guess they do. Fat Communion wafers for fat Catholics. I can let you have one, but that's all. Just one. *(She eats another Oreo. She takes the top off one and with great care she begins to apply the white cream filling as eye shadow to herself.)* When men leave us all we have left is our looks.

(GUSTAVITO embraces MERCY.)

MERCY: Sssh, Gustavito. Mercy, mercy me.

GUSTAVITO: Help me, I miss him so much.

MERCY: I don't want to hear this.

(GUSTAVITO stares at MERCY.)

MERCY: Yes I do.

GUSTAVITO: I know I'm not wrong.

MERCY: Gustavito.

GUSTAVITO: I'm going back someday.

(MERCY gives GUSTAVITO an Oreo.)

MERCY: Uh-huh.

GUSTAVITO: I don't know when I'm going—

MERCY: —but I'm going.

GUSTAVITO: Do you think God forgot about me?

MERCY: No.

GUSTAVITO: I made a promise with Him. It was my first one so I thought He would listen. You still think he will, right?

MERCY: Yeah, of course. I made a promise too. *(She points to her outfit.)* I want Esperanza to come back for Kiko.

(KIKO sits by the river, reading a telegram.)

MERCY: And she'll be just as she was when she left him. Like I saw them leave. Kiko came looking for me to say goodbye, but I hid. I could see the rice pelt them and I saw as he took her arm. He picked up Junior and hugged Esperanza. Then he kissed her like I've never seen anybody kiss anybody. And they got into a car and drove off. To the airport. New York. The next time I saw him he came to get me. But he wasn't smiling like that day with her so I didn't think I should smile either.

GUSTAVITO: Do you love him?

MERCY: I love him with pity. That's no way to love someone.

GUSTAVITO: And if he were to change.

MERCY: I'm never going to get the same smile I saw that day. Not from him.

(KIKO enters; he kisses GUSTAVITO's head.)

KIKO: Get your things together. We have to go back. Esperanza is dead. Her other family wants her buried in New York.

(MERCY exits. GUSTAVITO rises and as he heads to the church, KIKO exits while speaking.)

KIKO: We will only be going back for her wake and the funeral. Four days. That's it. You hear me? You hear me, Gustavito.

(GUSTAVITO enters the church.)

FATHER: We're not opened right now.

GUSTAVITO: Hey Father. Back from the dead, so to speak.

FATHER: Gustavito.

GUSTAVITO: Have I changed a lot? What do you think, Father?

FATHER: When did you get back?

GUSTAVITO: I came back for my mother's funeral. Not Mercy, Esperanza. My real mother. I haven't seen her yet. They could put any corpse in front of me and I would be expected to cry on cue.

FATHER: Whatever happened, Gustavito, she was your mother.

GUSTAVITO: Yes, Father, she was. Hey, it was an excuse to come back. I'm all cured now.

FATHER: I didn't know you were sick.

GUSTAVITO: You were the cause. First love, worst love.

FATHER: Gustavito.

GUSTAVITO: Gustavo.

FATHER: Gustavo. You're a young man now.

GUSTAVITO: Fifteen. You wanna sit?

FATHER: How's your family?

GUSTAVITO: Everybody's fine. Real happy, like always.

FATHER: Good. Does God still talk to you?

GUSTAVITO: I talk to Him.

FATHER: Does he listen?

GUSTAVITO: I'm here, aren't I? So who replaced me? Who became your altar boy?

FATHER: Domingo.

(GUSTAVITO *laughs*.)

GUSTAVITO: I knew it. Little prick. Excuse me. Before I left I was going to kill him. Seriously. Well, as seriously as a ten-year-old can think of something like that.

FATHER: As I recall you were a very serious ten-year-old.

GUSTAVITO: I didn't think you had any memory of me. So, first I was going to kill him then I decided it should be you. And me. I can't believe I'm confessing out here. Can we go to the confessional?

FATHER: This is fine.

GUSTAVITO: Please.

(FATHER *enters his space in the confessional and* GUSTAVITO *enters his.*)

GUSTAVITO: Forgive me Father for I have sinned. It has been five years since my last confession.

FATHER: Go ahead.

GUSTAVITO: You used to say, "Go ahead, my son."

FATHER: Go ahead, my son.

GUSTAVITO: So, you glad to see me? *(Silence)* Okay, where did I leave off? Oh yeah, I was going to kill us. I started hating you and me and I figured the pain would be better than the hate. But I didn't, so. Does that count as a sin? I thought it, but I didn't do it.

FATHER: Do you repent?

GUSTAVITO: I can't. Anyway, I don't have to. I'm over it. You.

FATHER: That's good.

GUSTAVITO: It's different for you. You never had anything to get over, right?

FATHER: You know, I could never find my rosary after you left.

GUSTAVITO: That's a shame. This little box was the safest place in the world to me. Where I first heard your voice, you remember?

FATHER: I really should get back.

GUSTAVITO: To what? I am over you.

(FATHER tries to leave the confessional; GUSTAVITO quickly follows him and grabs his wrist.)

GUSTAVITO: I am over you.

FATHER: I'm not going to fight with you, Gustavito. I did the right thing.

(GUSTAVITO slowly lets go of FATHER's wrist.)

GUSTAVITO: Did God tell you that? `Cause he didn't tell me. Gotta go. Oh, my penance.

FATHER: Please don't come here again.

GUSTAVITO: That ought to do it. *(He reaches into his pocket and pulls out FATHER's rosary.)* I was saving it for you. Here. *(FATHER does not move. GUSTAVITO dangles the rosary.)* Take it.

(FATHER does.)

GUSTAVITO: I wasn't going to keep it from you. It's yours. What's the Latin word for impossible? Never mind. I'm over you.

(GUSTAVITO exits. FATHER kneels, holding the rosary.)

FATHER: I've missed you.

(The funeral home. The Delgado family, all in black, sit watching the casket. KIKO wipes away a tear. He is the only one to do so.)

MERCY: *(To casket)* You still beat me, didn't you?

GUSTAVITO: *(To casket)* Wow, my lips. You have my lips. I've never seen them on anybody else. Well, I'm sorry you're dead. I mean I would be sorry if anybody was dead. I don't know you, Lady, but I'm sure you had your reasons for going. I hope I wasn't one of them. You didn't leave me any hints. You didn't leave me anything. Except your lips. Listen, if I lean over the coffin it's so they'll think I'm crying `cause I guess I should. But I can't. Sorry.

(GUSTAVITO *leans over the casket. At first he is just awkwardly over it, then he slowly embraces it. He rises and runs off.* JUNIOR *follows him.*)

KIKO: I am less angry than I thought I would be. I swore the next time I saw you I would kill you. Once again you got the better of me. So, I will never know why you walked out. Why you cheated on me. They don't know about that. I told everybody you just left. Were you happy after you left? I know you never were with me. I've tried harder with Mercy but you know I'm not a man of a lot of words. Junior's fine. He remembered you for a while. He thinks women always leave. For him they have. Gustavito. Gustavito is broken. And I don't know how to fix him. Sitting next to him and I don't know him anymore. Esperanza, if you can help at all with this. Don't forget me, Esperanza. And forgive me for whatever I did. *(He sits back down and tries to take* MERCY's *hand.)*

MERCY: What's the point? ...I want a little happiness, Kiko.

(Under MERCY's *speech* KIKO *will softly repeat the words "Caress me.")*

MERCY: A little for me, you know? I don't want to resent you anymore, Kiko. Your touch never belonged to me. You gave it to Consuelo, then Esperanza, how could I expect you to have any left over for me? I would like to see the boys every so often, if that's okay. And maybe someday we can see each other without you hating me.

*(*MERCY *rises.* KIKO *grabs her hand and kisses it. She exits.)*

KIKO: Mercedes.

(GUSTAVITO *enters the gay bar where* NORRY *once took him. The music that played there instantly plays again as he opens the door.*)

GUSTAVITO: Have you seen Norry? Have you seen Norry? Have you seen Norry? Have you seen Norry? Norry, where are you? I need you.

(FATHER *enters the penitent's side of a confessional. His side is lit while the other side remains dark.*)

FATHER: Forgive me Father for I have sinned. It has been an eternity since my last confession. I'm sorry, a week. God has placed a test in my path. Again. If I could understand His motives in doing this I might be better equipped to fight against it. He has placed me in the path of myself. I worry I will not have the strength to deny myself as I should. As He wills it. I need to be blind. I need to be immune.

GUSTAVITO: Cruise me, mother fucker. (*Dismissively*) Hi. (*Pause*) Pisces. (*Pause*) Oh, and you? (*Pause*) Neat. No. (*Pause*) No. (*Pause*) No. Yeah, you can buy me a beer. I'm old enough. How old are you? (*Pause*) I figured. No, I said "It's sunny out today." (*Pause*) Okay, so it's sunny out tonight. (*Pause*) My name is... Junior. (*Pause*) Uh, thank you, but I don't dance.... I have a heart condition. Nice meeting you, too.

FATHER: Any chance of me getting a sign from God? I don't mean to be disrespectful. I just feel I've been abandoned by Him. You're in that little black box because you want to be, right? That must make all the difference in the world.

(GUSTAVITO *touches the back of his neck, and he bites his lower lip; in short, he does everything he learned from* NORRY, *all to no avail. He comes across more as desperate than sexy. He spots someone.*)

GUSTAVITO: Hi. *(His eyes follow the person as he leaves.)* Bye. *(He smells under his arm pits.)*

FATHER: Would God be terribly upset if I were happy? No, you ask Him. I don't think He wants to speak to me.

(The Delgado family living room in New York. Everything is as we last saw it. The wedding dress is still on the dummy. There are old blood stains on parts of it and the pieces that were ripped off have not been replaced. JUNIOR, *using his key, enters. He looks around a bit before* NORRY *enters.)*

JUNIOR: You didn't change the locks.

NORRY: Did Mercy come back with you?

JUNIOR: They told me you took over our apartment.

NORRY: I pay the rent. It's mine now.

JUNIOR: Hey, I don't care. *(He walks up to the wedding dress.)* You kept my blood. That's sweet.

NORRY: So, is Mercy back?

JUNIOR: You look different.

NORRY: I'm going for a new look. Norry Lite.

JUNIOR: Look, I came here to say I was sorry for the way I treated you.

NORRY: And just how did you treat me?

JUNIOR: Like shit.

NORRY: Today my son you are a man.

JUNIOR: You did okay by me. I mean, I don't know why, but... How did you get Mercy to fall in love with you?

NORRY: You think she's in love with me?

JUNIOR: If...if you wanted to make somebody fall in love with you, what would you do?

NORRY: I don't know how to do that.

JUNIOR: Yes, you do.

NORRY: Junior, I'm flattered. But one of us would have to be sedated. Just buy me a little love trinket and we'll call it even.

JUNIOR: Not you, you freak.

NORRY: Hey!

JUNIOR: I'm sorry...I'm sorry. There's...somebody I love, but I don't think they love me. I figured if you made Mercy fall in love with you, you could do anything.

NORRY: Are you sure it's not me? I've had straight boys fall in love with me before. I'm probably the first queer you ever talked to without using your fists.

JUNIOR: I'm not in love with you. You looked better in a dress.

NORRY: Maybe you would, too.

(JUNIOR *turns to leave.* NORRY *stops him.*)

NORRY: Okay, okay, okay. Do something romantic for them. Serenade...her. Nobody does that anymore.

JUNIOR: Like in the middle of the street? No, I don't think so.

NORRY: She'll love it.

JUNIOR: Gimme something else.

NORRY: No. You want love to be easy? Well, it's not. Go out there and make a fool of yourself like the rest of us. Take the leap or get the hell out of the way and let the rest of us commit suicide.

JUNIOR: What if I die?

NORRY: You die. And guess what? It doesn't get any easier the next time.

JUNIOR: Mercy will be at the Rosado Funeral Home on Tremont. Six p m. We're even now, okay? *(He exits.)*

NORRY: If you say so.

(NORRY *and* MERCY *meet again; he is dressed like a man. She in a black version of her "promise" outfit. He sees her walking by and stops her.*)

NORRY: Mercedes.

MERCY: Norry? (*She circles him.*)

NORRY: I'm sort of trying to be Norberto now. Simple, tasteful. Plain.

MERCY: Plain?

NORRY: Plain me. And you? (*He circles her.*)

MERCY: I made a promise.

NORRY: To what? Disappear?

MERCY: It doesn't matter anymore.

NORRY: Love your earring.

MERCY: A peacock gave it to me.

(NORRY *produces a small bouquet of violets from his jacket.*)

NORRY: Here. These are for you. I know you like them.

MERCY: I like them because someone gave them to me. It wasn't you.

NORRY: No. No, it wasn't.

MERCY: Junior tells me you took over our apartment?

NORRY: Yes, I did. It's just the way you left it.

MERCY: Tell me, is the wedding dress still there?

NORRY: Of course.

MERCY: And it's still not finished?

NORRY: It'll never be finished. I tried to finish it but I don't know how to sew, Mercedes. Do you hear what I'm telling you? I don't know how to sew. And at this late stage in my life I don't know if I could even learn to thread the needle.

MERCY: It's okay.

NORRY: I want to make you happy and if my sewing would do that I would try with all my might, but needle and thread are not what I'm about. That's why I searched you out a million years ago.

(Silence)

MERCY: Two virgins.

NORRY: Two virgins.

MERCY: Do you want to learn?

NORRY: To sew?

MERCY: To sew.

NORRY: I...

(MERCY kisses NORRY.)

MERCY: Your hands are still softer than mine.

NORRY: You didn't expect me to throw out thirty-eight years of skin care products, did you?

(Pause. MERCY puts NORRY's earring on him.)

MERCY: This belongs to you. I borrowed it and you must always return what you borrow. And I *want* you to have it back. It looks good on you.

NORRY: I can't change who I am, Mercy, and I don't want to, but I want to love you.

MERCY: ...Can I stay with you for a while?

NORRY: Until we finish the wedding dress.

(MERCY and NORRY shake hands.)

MERCY & NORRY: Deal.

(JUNIOR enters. He whistles a verse of I'm Through With Love as MERCY and NORRY exit. He carries a brown paper bag with a bottle in it. He takes a long drink and sits on the stoop and begins to cry.)

JUNIOR: I'm fucked.

(GUSTAVITO *enters church and spots* FATHER.)

GUSTAVITO: Hi, Father. I'm going back to P R today. *(He holds up his hands in a truce sign.)* I just came to say `bye.

FATHER: `Bye.

(Silence. GUSTAVITO *initiates an awkward handshake.)*

FATHER: I'll pray for you.

GUSTAVITO: Yeah, I'll pray for you, too. Betcha I pray longer than you do.

FATHER: No fair, He listens to you.

GUSTAVITO: He used to.

FATHER: He will again.

(Silence. GUSTAVITO *turns to leave.)*

GUSTAVITO: If He does maybe He can tell me why you laid there on the floor and let Kiko beat you? Why you begged for forgiveness as if we had done something wrong?

FATHER: Because we did.

GUSTAVITO: What I felt...feel for you is not wrong and what you feel for me is not wrong.

FATHER: I don't have any right to feel anything for you. Where are we supposed to go? What are we supposed to do? Gustavito, I know the world that we live in, there is no place for us there.

GUSTAVITO: Am I the only one in love here? *(Silence)* Just tell me, am I the only one in love?

FATHER: Before I met you, I can honestly say I have never loved anything. Or anyone. Not the way you do. I envy people who say they would die without something. To die of desire. You were away from me for five years and it didn't change your obsession.

GUSTAVITO: I'm not obsessed.

FATHER: What would you call it?

GUSTAVITO: I'm in love.

FATHER: Gustavito, I would give half of my life if things were different, but they're not.

GUSTAVITO: Then will you wait for me if I wait for you? *(Silence)* At ten years old I was ready to do battle with Kiko for you. I was willing to take on my whole entire world for you, but I can't do this by myself anymore. I can't. I can't. *(Turns to leave)* I won't. *(He exits.)*

FATHER: God?

(GUSTAVITO enters NORRY's apartment.)

NORRY: Life would be so much simpler if one could fall in love with the "right" person.

GUSTAVITO: Tell me about it.

NORRY: I'm a good man, an honorable man, but am I her man?

GUSTAVITO: Do you love her?

NORRY: ...Yeah. My dear, how did this happen?

GUSTAVITO: You know, sometimes when things really got bad for me I would try to imagine what you would do and it would make me smile.

NORRY: You were laughing at me?

GUSTAVITO: Never. I gotta go back.

NORRY: You can stay with Mercy and me.

GUSTAVITO: I don't want to risk running into him. You know he really does love me in his own way.

NORRY: Uh-huh, that was tired even before it got out your mouth.

GUSTAVITO: I would do anything if he would take me back.

NORRY: Back where? You haven't been anyplace.

GUSTAVITO: Why do goodbyes have to hurt so much?

NORRY: Goodbyes are a piece of cake. It's the hellos that leave the scars. *(He holds him gently and kisses him on the forehead.)* Nobody falls in love faster than a virgin. And that includes forever-young drag queens.

(From outside they hear singing.)

JUNIOR: *(Voice only)*
I'm through with love
I'll never fall again
Said I'm through with love
La la la la la la
For I must have you or no one
And so I'm through with love

(NORRY looks up. He goes to the fire escape.)

GUSTAVITO: What's that?

NORRY: The most romantic thing that never happened to me.

GUSTAVITO: Is it for you?

NORRY: It's on loan.

(GUSTAVITO exits. NORRY climbs out on the fire escape.)

JUNIOR: I'm through with love
I'll never fall again
Said I'm through with love
La la la la la la
For I must have you or no one
And so I'm through with—

(JUNIOR and NORRY face each other. JUNIOR runs off.)

NORRY: All I did was be nice to him, and now I've gone and confused him.

(On the street)

GUSTAVITO: Hey.

JUNIOR: Just don't say nothing, okay? I'm gonna get married.

GUSTAVITO: To who?

JUNIOR: I said not to say nothing. *(He makes a fist as if to hit him.)* Zoraya the second. Actually her name is Nydia but she said it's okay for me to call her Zoraya.

GUSTAVITO: Do you love her?

(JUNIOR casually punches GUSTAVITO in the jaw, hard. GUSTAVITO falls to the ground. JUNIOR continues, very matter of factly.)

JUNIOR: She is marrying me to get out of her house. Her parents are too strict. She told me, so it's cool.

GUSTAVITO: Do you sing to her?

JUNIOR: I don't have to. *(He gets down on the same level as GUSTAVITO.)* This is strictly a no-risk, no-commitment situation. And when she leaves it won't hurt. At all. Thinking ahead. That's what you should be doing.

GUSTAVITO: So why were you singing to Norry?

(JUNIOR locks him in a hammerlock, squeezing the air out of him.)

JUNIOR: One thing you have to decide is what you're willing to give up. I know my limitations and I can sense you're getting dangerously close to yours.

(He releases GUSTAVITO, who collapses, gasping for air.)

JUNIOR: I'll get married. I'll have a kid. Fuck, I'll kill Norry if I have to but I'll be okay. This I swear to you.

GUSTAVITO: And Zoraya?

JUNIOR: Ah, she never did give me the time of day. God invented love to punish people. *(He suddenly stops. He*

"sees" Zoraya. He waves to her.) Hey, Zoraya. *(Sings)* For
I must have you or no one—

JUNIOR & NORRY: And so I'm through with love.

*(JUNIOR looks from Zoraya, to NORRY's fire escape, and back
to Zoraya again.)*

JUNIOR: Oh, fuck. Stereo.

(KIKO goes to NORRY, who is still on the fire escape.)

KIKO: How do I compete with you?

NORRY: You don't.

KIKO: *(Pulls out a small bouquet of violets)* What do I do
with these?

NORRY: Tell her.

KIKO: Someone told me she already has herself another
man. Delicate, gentle, some would even say beautiful.

NORRY: Some would. I'm not holding her here with
any threats. She's here because she wants to be here.

(MERCY takes the wedding dress off the dummy.)

KIKO: You're not afraid of me.

NORRY: Let her see you with the violets in your hand.
Let her know you were her secret admirer.

KIKO: I couldn't do that.

(MERCY takes off her habit dress.)

NORRY: Couldn't. What a big word.

*(KIKO brings the violets to his heart. NORRY goes inside.
JUNIOR enters the street, carrying his bottle of malt liquor.
He sits on the floor. From his pocket he takes out a deck of
cards and begins to play solitaire, in the same manner that
KIKO did.)*

JUNIOR: When did I become my father?

(MERCY *puts on the wedding dress. She reaches out for* NORRY.)

MERCY: It's still not finished. Come, my peacock.

(KIKO *is standing outside the door of* NORRY's *apartment.*)

(FATHER *is performing a wedding ceremony.* GUSTAVITO *enters, standing in the back of the church.*)

FATHER: ...here before your friends and family. Do you, do you Jorge take Carmen as your lawfully wedded wife from this day forward, to have and to hold in sickness and in health as long as you both shall live?

GUSTAVITO: *(Softly)* I do.

FATHER: And. And do you Carmen take Gustavito, I'm sorry, take Jorge as you lawfully wedded husband from this day forward, to have and to hold in sickness and in health as long as you both shall live? Can you do that, Carmen? *(Pause)* Yes. Of course you can. You love each other. Here, before God, I now declare you husband and wife. You may kiss the bride.

(GUSTAVITO *takes a step forward and the* FATHER *takes one back.*)

GUSTAVITO: I'm sorry I wasn't born earlier. I'm sorry I bother you. I'm sorry I cause you pain. Hey, Father, which is the bigger sin? Yours or mine?

(*Lights down, then up on* GUSTAVITO, *who comes up behind* KIKO *at apartment door.*)

GUSTAVITO: Hey, we leaving or what?

(KIKO *nods. He begins to trace a heart on the door using the violets.*)

GUSTAVITO: It's just you and me, huh, Kiko?

(KIKO *places the violets on the floor outside the door. He puts his arm around* GUSTAVITO. *They both stare at each other.* KIKO *removes his arm. They both put their hands in their pockets.)*

(MERCY *looks at* NORRY. *She shakes her head, sits him down, and pulls out a make-up kit. She begins to apply make-up to his face. He takes her hand, kisses it, and begins to apply make-up to her.)*

(KIKO *goes to where* JUNIOR *is playing cards and moves one of them for him.)*

KIKO: A spade is a spade.

(JUNIOR *collects his cards and turns away from* KIKO.)

JUNIOR: It's called solitaire.

(GUSTAVITO *and* KIKO *begin to walk. Enter* FATHER.)

FATHER: Gustavito.

(GUSTAVITO *and* KIKO *stop walking.* KIKO *continues.)*

KIKO: Come on.

FATHER: Gustavito.

KIKO: Come on, we're gonna miss the plane.

(GUSTAVITO *is standing between the two fathers. He looks at* FATHER *and shakes his head. He walks toward* KIKO.)

FATHER: If you wait for me I'll wait for you.

(GUSTAVITO *turns to* FATHER.)

FATHER: If you wait for me I'll wait for you.

KIKO: If you go to him I'll kill him.

(GUSTAVITO *takes* KIKO's *hands and places them on his throat.)*

GUSTAVITO: Then you have to kill me. `Cause I love him. To your face, Kiko, I love him.

(KIKO *embraces* GUSTAVITO.)

KIKO: If you come with me I'll close my eyes to everything. You will never tell and I'll never know.

GUSTAVITO: I want you to know, Kiko. I need you to know.

(KIKO kisses GUSTAVITO and exits.)

FATHER: I don't want to be afraid anymore.

(The stage darkens as the cross begins to glow.)

GUSTAVITO: And I don't want to have to apologize or deny or look down.

(FATHER nods and takes GUSTAVITO's hand. They kneel before the cross.)

FATHER: Father, I want you to meet Gustavito.

GUSTAVITO: He knows me.

FATHER: Father, I want you to meet me.

END OF PLAY

www.ingramcontent.com/pod-product-compliance
Lightning Source LLC
Chambersburg PA
CBHW052208090426
42741CB00010B/2455